There Was a Young Girl from Verona

A Limerick Cycle Based on the
Complete Dramatic Works of Shakespeare

by
Max Gutmann

with illustrations by Jerry Seltzer

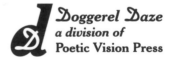

Doggerel Daze
a division of
Poetic Vision Press

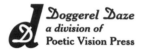

Doggerel Daze
a division of
Poetic Vision Press

10144 Riedel Place
Cupertino, CA 95014
www.ddaze.com
info@ddaze.com

ISBN 0-9722820-0-9

Graphic design by András Király, Toboz Kft.
Cover design by Jerry Seltzer.
Creative Consultants: Harriet Eckstein, András Király
Special thanks to Gabriella László.

There Was a Young Girl From Verona first appeared in *Tundra: The Journal of the Short Poem*. Excerpts have been published by Wells College Press, and in *Light Quarterly*.

Cataloging-in-Publication Data

Gutmann, Max.
There was a young girl from Verona : a limerick cycle based on the complete dramatic works of Shakespeare/ Max Gutmann.
P. cm.
ISBN 0-9722820-0-9
1. Limericks. 2. Shakespeare, William, 1564-1616. I. Title.
808.817'5—dc21
Library of Congress Control Number: 2002111068

for John Ridland

TABLE OF CONTENTS

The Comedies

A Midsummer Night's Dream

In *dementia tremens* Titania,
A disease which attacks women's crania,
    The afflicted young lass
    Falls in love with an ass.
It's a terribly prevalent mania.

The Merchant of Venice

Although moderns feel Shylock the Jew
Receives treatment far worse than his due,
   In *this* play, the thing's
    To sort out the rings
So the lovers can have a good screw.

Twelfth Night

Growled a hard-drinking actor named Earp,
"My director's a prissy old twerp!
    Even censors the bard,
    And I'll tell you, it's hard
Playing someone called Sir Toby Burp!"

14

Much Ado About Nothing

For changeable men, sigh no more;
They've one foot in sea, one on shore,
    So be blithe and be bonny,
    Sing Hey nonny, nonny,
And give 'em a kick in the oar.

As You Like It

From this day, motley's all I will wear,
For I met me a fool who spake fair:
    He said, "Now it is ten,
    But I still recall when
It was nine. Quite a tale hangs right there."

The Two Gentlemen of Verona

"No use!" mourned Lucetta. "My trade
Is doomed to be thankless. A maid
   Can be witty, insightful,
   In all ways delightful,
But still it's the lady gets laid."

The Taming of the Shrew

When you set about taming your mate,
Put your foot down before it's too late.
    If you don't, you will see
    That the tamer is she.
(Other husbands will commiserate.)

Love's Labour's Lost

In Navarre, there's a strict, sexless diet,
And this statute makes sure all stand by it:
    Any woman about
    Has her tongue cut right out,
Which is harsh, but ensures peace and quiet.

The Merry Wives of Windsor

From the error of Abraham Slender
Take a lesson: to love just surrender.
   If your first choice is vexed,
    Simply take up the next;
Don't get bogged down in details, like gender.

EPHESVS

SYRACVSE

The Comedy of Errors

For this farce, an abundance of twos is
The device with which Shakespeare amuses:
Twins in looks and in speech,
With a sister for each,
And twin servants (with twin sets of bruises).

Troilus and Cressida

Troilus crooned to his love, "Darling Cressid,
I feel certain our union is blesséd,
   For you're passionate, true
   As an angel, and you
Could outclass Aphrodite undresséd."

All's Well That Ends Well

"I refuse to be Helena's prize,"
 Pouted Bertram. "I'll use my own eyes,
  For a man of my worth
  Needs a wife of high birth
(Or at least one with slenderer thighs)."

Measure for Measure

To her brother, the chaste Isabella
Said, "Aw, look at the sunny side, fella:
 For a nice final meal
  They can bring you some veal—
And no worries about salmonella!"

The Histories

King John

Though King John, without doubt, was no saint,
You could say he'd a valid complaint
    When he hollered, "Confound
    It, stop messin' around.
Either Arthur is dead or he ain't!"

Richard II

Uncle Gaunt's final words were a warning
Which the king showed ill judgment in scorning.
When Gaunt's last groan was groaned,
Richard seized all he'd owned,
An unfortunate method of mourning.

Henry IV, Part 1

If just holidays filled the whole year,
Then we soon would grow tired of cheer
    And to sport would so irk
    That we'd just as soon work.
But they don't, so let's have some more beer.

Henry IV, Part 2

Hooting, "Nothing succeeds like succession!
Long live thievery, lies and aggression!"
    Falstaff flies to his pal,
    Newly crowned good King Hal,
But he'll soon do his door-nail impression.

Henry V

What the history book seldom teaches
About one of King Hal's famous speeches
    Is he borrowed a phrase
    From his profligate days:
"Hardy gals, once more into my breeches."

Henry VI, Part 1

Valiant Talbot combats fiends of Hell
In the person of Joan la Pucelle.
    At Bordeaux, Talbot dies;
    La Pucelle, of course, fries;
Henry doesn't die yet. (Might as well.)

Henry VI, Part 2

"Suffolk, dear, I don't think I can cope,"
Margaret seethed. "Henry's just a big dope!
    With his beads all the time,
    And his saints, and his—I'm
Not the queen, I'm the wife of the Pope!"

Henry VI, Part 3

Richard Third is a notable villain,
And his speech in *3 Henry's* quite chillin':
    "There are men in my way
     And I'm ugly, but—hey,
I'm a whiz at deceivin' and killin'."

Richard III

Being courted by Richard the Third,
Lady Anne took the man at his word;
    Thus the woman pursued
    Was successfully wooed,
Married, taken to bed, and interred.

Henry VIII

Though Wolsey and Katherine take dives,
A cast of new people survives;
    But to me the odd trait
    Of the play *Henry 8*
Is: where are the other four wives?

The Romances

The Tempest

"Brave new world!" shouts excited Miranda,
With a rapture we all understand: a
    Girl who'd never caught sight
    Of a man *would* delight
In a jaw line, a biceps, a hand, a...

The Winter's Tale

If you exit pursued by a bear,
There's a chance you'll escape by a hair.
   (There is also a chance
   You'll grow moss in your pants,
But they're both of them awfully rare.)

The Two Noble Kinsmen

Shakespeare's *Two Noble Kinsmen*'s the best
Of the plays for the critics to test:
    In each article they
    Laud the fine parts, and say
That John Fletcher—that hack—wrote the rest.

Cymbeline

Feeble Cloten, the son of the queen,
Can't make twenty from two and eighteen,
    Tell a duck from a cow,
    Or quite figure out how
To consume an unpeeled tangerine.

Pericles, Prince of Tyre

This new whore stands in need of correction.
She quotes scripture and verse to perfection,
    Which is good for the soul,
    But it sure takes its toll
On maintaining a fellow's erection!

The Tragedies

Hamlet

Here's the question: to be or to not?
Is it nobler to suffer or rot?
    For time's whips and time's scorn
    Are too great to be born.
On the other hand, death's not so hot.

King Lear

Feeling Goneril, 'Delia, and Regan
Far too greedy and sly and intriguin',
Old Lear gritted his teeth
And retired to the heath
As a radical communist vegan.

MacBeth

Harried Mac needs a way he can nurse
His bad conscience (a horrible curse
   When you've murdered a king),
   So, to lighten the sting,
He finds new things to do that are worse.

Titus Andronicus

In the bowdlerized version of *Titus*,
Since to lop hands and tongues would affright us,
    To replace these travails
    Titus pares off his nails
And Lavinia gets laryngitis.

Coriolanus

The Roman showed Coriolanus
Ingratitude really quite heinous.
    Snarled the general, "I am,
    For revenge, gonna jam
This forty-stone sword up your nose."

Timon of Athens

"Oh, the agony! Coming so near!"
Timon moaned as he sobbed in his beer.
 "With a realm to give up
 And a fool and a coup-
Le of daughters, I could have been Lear!"

Julius Ceasar

"There's a tide, Cassius, great men have found,"
Noble Brutus was heard to expound,
   "Which if taken at swell
    Makes grand projects go well,"
So they both of them took it and drowned.

Antony and Cleopatra

According to Queen Cleopatra,

Her taste wasn't really all that re-

Cherché: "Just a villa

And frock. (Say chinchilla?)

Perhaps a few pearls.

And some eunuchs and girls.

Oh, of course a small barge.

(Sixty footer too large?)"

Et catra, et catra, et catra.

Othello

The truth is that doomed Desdemona,
Because her sad fate had been shown her,
    Slept with Cassio, Bill,
    A Brit tourist named Jill,
And both of those gents from Verona.

Romeo and Juliet

If her lover were only a rose,
Juliet's famous axiom goes,
    He could have any name
    And would still smell the same—
But it's no fun to fuck one of those.

MAX GUTMANN has contributed to more than three dozen journals and magazines, including *Cricket, Light Quarterly, The Formalist, Tundra,* and a number of publications with *Review* in their titles.

JERRY SELTZER is an illustrator and cartoonist currently residing in Savannah, Georgia. A lover of all things medieval, he is the creator of the nationally syndicated cartoon strip, Gunchello. The strip, about a wizard and a dragon, is his pride and joy. Jerry draws political cartoons, also in syndication. His political leanings are summed up in the phrase "compassionate common sense." He recieved his B.F.A. from the Savannah College of Art and Design and is working toward his M.F.A. so that he might teach others the art of cartooning. To contact Jerry, visit www.gunchello.com.

DOGGEREL DAZE ACKNOWLEDGEMENTS

Doggerel Daze has received advice, materials, time, and energy from many people, and is particularly grateful to Judit Barna, Maryann Brown, Harriet Eckstein, Fred Gutmann, Rochelle Gutmann, Patricia Hamilton, Ágnes Hompasz, X. J. Kennedy, András Király, Gabriella László, Gábor Árpád Németh, Brigitta Orbán, John Ridland, and János Simon.

QUICK ORDER FORM

Doggerel Daze; 10144 Riedel Place; Cupertino, CA 95014

For information on current Doggerel Daze titles, visit us at **www.ddaze.com** or write to **info@ddaze.com**

Customer Name _____

Street Address _____

City, State, Zip _____

Please enclose check or money order.

Book title (and number ordered, if more than one)	Price
California residents add 7.5% sales tax	
Shipping (see below)	
Total	

Domestic shipping charges: Media rate: $3 total for 1-2 books; $4 total for 3-6 books.
Priority mail (1-3 days): $5 for 1 book.

Contact us for international shipping charges or priority shipping rates for more than 1 book; these vary depending on your location.